How to Buy a House 2 Years or Less After Bankruptcy Discharge

Pria J. Jackson, MBA

www.afteryourbankruptcy.com

P. Tronell Subsidiaries, LLC

ptronellsub@gmail.com

Because of the dynamic nature of the internet, web addresses or links referred to in this guide may no longer be valid.

ISBN-13: 978-1-7341148-2-9

ISBN: 978-0-578-49405-0 (e-book)

*Photos obtained from Shutterstock.com and Pexels.com.

Other books in this series are available at
www.afteryourbankruptcy.com

Credit Repair: How to Get Your Credit Score to 700 in 2 Years or Less After Bankruptcy

Credit Repair: How to Buy a Vehicle 30 Days or Less After Bankruptcy Discharge

Disclaimer

The views stated in this work are solely those of the author and do not necessarily reflect the beliefs of the publisher. The publisher disclaims any responsibility for the opinions.

The author and publisher do not make any guarantees and release all liability for risk, harm, or losses resulting from applying data contained in this text. You are encouraged to seek advice from a real estate broker, lawyer, or mortgage professional. The accuracy of the information presented is not guaranteed.

This book is intended to assist with your home purchase after bankruptcy. It is not meant to be your sole reference during the buying process.

Acknowledgment

I thank everyone who has supported my endeavors throughout the years. I would especially like to acknowledge my mother and father, Troy and Nellie Mae Groover, who are now resting in Heaven.

Thank you for being supportive and providing sound advice. "Nothing beats a failure, but a try," are words which still resonates.

Rest in peace, Troy Stanley and Phillip Scott.

Prelude

I, like you, have had to recover from bankruptcy and reclaim my credit life. Yes, there are hundreds of books written on this very subject. But I bet that most of the authors do not share my unique experiences. What distinguishes me from the pack?

(1) As mentioned, I have been up, close, and personal with bankruptcy and recovery.

(2) After two failed businesses, Chapter 7 was my only recourse.

(3) During my years as a Real Estate and Mortgage professional, I coached clients on how to improve their credit scores.

(4) I have held many first-time home buying seminars, which included information on credit repair and bankruptcy recovery.

(5) I am educated in business, which includes having an MBA.

(6) I once worked as a Financial Representative, again discussing credit with clients.

My work experiences and college degrees did not shield me from financial woes and eventual bankruptcy relief. However, today, I can share with you how I have recovered to owning property in Florida and Georgia.

I am not where I want to be, but I am well on the way. Let me state that I do not know it all, no one person does, but education and life experiences were all that were needed to achieve my goals.

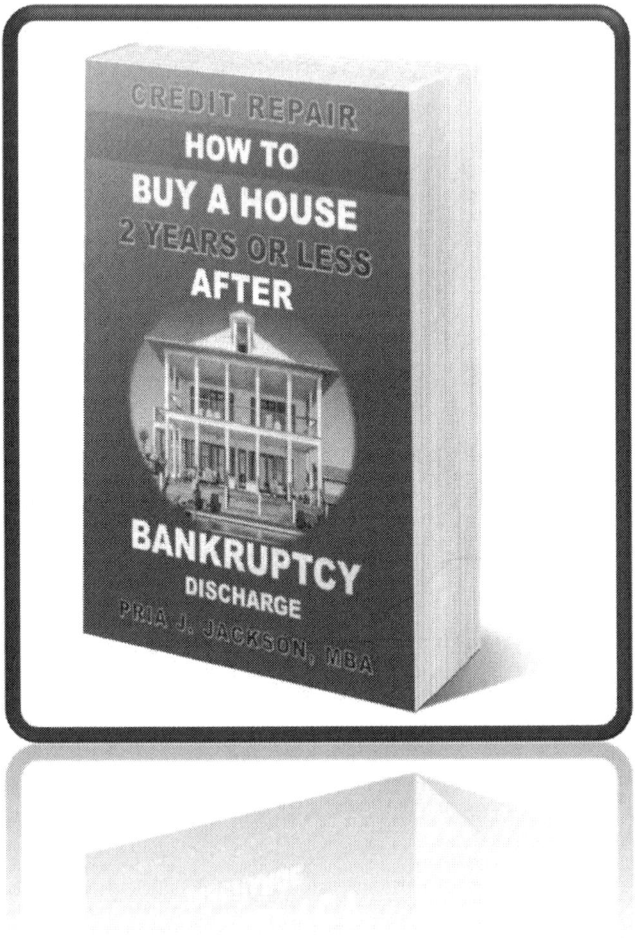
CREDIT REPAIR
HOW TO
BUY A HOUSE
2 YEARS OR LESS
AFTER
BANKRUPTCY
DISCHARGE
PRIA J. JACKSON, MBA

Table of Contents

DISCHARGED

Chapter 1

Introduction

Having to file bankruptcy is an unfortunate event. But we do what we must to regain control of our credit and financial lives. After the entire bankruptcy ordeal, individuals often want to buy a new house.

However, for whatever reason, the thought after bankruptcy is 'I will not be able to do anything requiring credit for ten years.' Nothing could be further from the truth. You can buy a home in two years or less - if you have a game plan.

Going through bankruptcy can be disheartening. It sets your credit and financial life back a bit. But the reality is, as your discharge ages, your situation improves; especially if you take the time to restore your credit profile.

Once you complete the reestablishment process and add new accounts, your score rises from its bottomed-out position. It is possible to have a credit number of 700 within two years; even with the bankruptcy still showing on your report.

As for buying a home, once you complete the credit repair and reestablishment rituals, it is possible to purchase twelve months after Chapter 13 and 24 months after Chapter 7. But guess what? Depending on the reason for Chapter 7, you could qualify to buy one year after discharge.

However, this is harder to accomplish and requires certain verifiable circumstances. Twenty-four months is more probable.

The home loan programs that are most forgiving for bankruptcy discharge are FHA (Federal Housing Authority) and VA (Veterans Administration). Many banks, credit unions, and mortgage brokers offer them. The key is to start working on your home buying goal as soon as possible.

This book provides a path that can make this happen. Within a matter of months, you can be lounging on a patio, sun porch, or deck -

enjoying the view from your backyard. It is very doable, so follow along and let me get you there.

Chapter 2

Can I 'Really' Buy After 2 Years?

As previously stated, Chapter 7 filers can qualify for a mortgage under FHA and VA programs two years after discharge. Chapter 13 filers can buy after 12 months.

It all depends on credit and financial positions. Again, discharged Chapter 7's may also be eligible for FHA after 12 months if non-repeatable circumstances caused the bankruptcy.

The ability to buy after bankruptcy depends on:

- ✓ Credit repair;
- ✓ Credit reestablishment;
- ✓ Credit score;
- ✓ Down payment;
- ✓ Cash reserves in a bank or investment account;

- ✓ Discharge being two years old (one in some cases);
- ✓ Two-years employment/self-employment;
- ✓ Income and Debt-to-Income.

Although this list is short, these are not the only requirements - just the main ones. Tackling the items can put you on track to buying a new home. If not your dream home, something close to it – even brand new if that is your preference.

CREDIT REPAIR
GUIDE
1ST STEP
AFTER
NKRUPTCY
CHARGE
N, MBA

Chapter 3

Repair Your Credit

The first step of your home buying objective is credit repair. About 45 days after discharge, you should begin updating your credit profile. This period provides enough time for the court to report your new status as 'discharged.' The update is critical.

Repair

Start the restoration process by retrieving a copy of my guide *1st Step After Bankruptcy Discharge*. The handbook can be downloaded, free of charge, from the website www.afteryourbankruptcy.com. It is also available at www.amazon.com for a small fee.

The booklet is a quick read that takes less than 20 minutes to complete. However, implementing the concepts is much longer. Again, retrieve this free reference and begin following the steps immediately.

1st Step After Bankruptcy Discharge provides detailed instructions on how to identify errors on the three credit reports. It gives direction on disputing incorrect data, as well as, offers correspondence examples.

Follow the guide, pull the reports, and dispute any inaccuracies. Not only will this repair your credit and assist with increasing the scores, but it provides a better negotiating position when making future purchases. Taking the time to address issues is very important.

The next step after the repair is reestablishment.

Reestablishment

For scores to increase, you must establish new accounts. I am aware that immediately after bankruptcy, the thought may be to protect yourself from ever going through it again. This decision could be to 'not apply for any new credit' so that future debt problems are avoided. Although this sounds good, it may not be practical.

Any future large purchases require the use of credit for most individuals. Very few people can buy an automobile or house for cash. Even some car and home repairs can be so costly that they too require debt.

The key is to reestablish yourself slowly and meticulously. Have a strategy. If you are reading this book, then the plan is to buy a house.

A score of 620 is needed to achieve your home purchase goal; possibly 640. Why one of these scores? Because you will then be able to qualify with most lenders; as well as comparison shop.

Loan programs are not all black and white; extenuating circumstances can prevail. Requirements vary between lenders. For instance, one creditor may accept a 620 score for approval; another may not. It is a guessing game. In this book, I have tried to present scenarios acceptable by most underwriters.

For clarification, if you decide <u>not</u> to establish new accounts, you may still be able to buy. If two years after bankruptcy, you have no scores nor trade lines, it is possible for the lender to manually approve your mortgage application. In this case, the bank then requests and evaluates documented receipts from:

- Rent, utilities, or cell phone payments;
- Business-owned child-care expenses;
- School tuition, auto lease, or personal medical bills.

However, consider the rebuilding route. As stated earlier, if a large home or auto repair is needed - you may want to spread the payments - rather than fork up a large lump-sum.

Just recently, I had to replace my entire heating and air system. I was able to spread the payments over 24 months, interest-free.

Had I not restored my credit; I would have had to pay the entire amount from my savings. In this scenario, I still got to buy the system – same as cash; without having to raid my bank account.

Just as the book *1st Step After Bankruptcy Discharge* can assist with the credit repair process, *How to Get Your Score to 700 in 2 years or Less After Bankruptcy* goes one step further and provides the reestablishment method.

Again, to obtain a copy visit www.afteryourbankruptcy.com. If you decide to purchase *Credit Score to 700,* there is no need to download the other one.

To restore credit, start slowly with secured debt then eventually move to unsecured. If your house and car were reaffirmed during the bankruptcy, then these will be instrumental in moving credit scores in the right direction. Most importantly, pay bills on time, and keep any open credit balances to 30% or less of the approved amounts.

Notes

Chapter 4

Professional Assistance

After all credit files have been updated, start thinking about the mortgage process. It is at this point that you should seek a loan officer who has experience with government deals.

Be very upfront with the professional and let her know that you are on a two-year mission. Explain about the bankruptcy and how you have already started repairing your credit. Be honest; these individuals are not salaried but commissioned. She will not receive any income until after the loan closes - two years later.

Some loan officers may not have the time, but others will be happy to assist. Although the purchase may be delayed for two years, you do have acquaintances and can be a referral source in the interim. Hopefully, you can find the ideal professional at the beginning of this journey. In the meantime, I am providing the basics so that you can understand the overall process.

Notes

FHA & VA
Requirements

Chapter 5

Mortgage Loan Programs

A mortgage is a loan secured by real estate - homes, buildings, or land. The primary programs are FHA, VA, and conventional. There are other categories such as jumbo, subprime, and hard money.

However, the focus of this book is FHA and VA. Why? Because these permit purchases within two years after bankruptcy and provide competitive interest rates.

The U.S. Department of Housing and Urban Development guarantees FHA (Federal Housing Authority) loans; VA by the Veterans Administration. With these programs, the lender gets his money even if you default. However, the government does not issue loans; it just assures them.

Government-backed programs are more forgiving than conventional. They have different parameters. From the type of borrower to closing cost contribution – and everything in-between, the loan requirements are unique.

FHA Requirements

1. Type of borrower

The loan is available for all borrowers.

2. Income Verification

Hourly workers - The lender calculates income by evaluating the most recent 30 days of paystubs. They also examine the past two income tax returns, especially if bonuses and overtime were earned.

Salaried - The last 30 days of pay-stubs are required. The bank requests two years of tax documents, as well.

Self-Employed or 1099 Contractor – The first condition is that you have been in this category for at least the past couple of years. The last two tax filings will verify this status. The qualification amount is the average of your adjusted gross incomes from the two tax statements.

If there were deductions, let your loan officer determine the qualifying income – especially in the early stages of the process. Again, make sure that you hire a mortgage professional who has FHA or VA experience; else she may douse your home ownership dream by falsely stating that you must wait four years before making a purchase.

3. Mortgage Insurance

Mortgage insurance is required - upfront and monthly. Individuals must pay an average upfront premium of 1.75% (which can be financed) and a monthly premium of .85% of the loan sum. These percentages, which can change at any point, are based on a qualifying loan amount of 96.5% with a 3.5% down-payment.

Mortgage insurance protects the lender if a person defaults on the loan. It is required when the down-payment is less than 20%.

This type of coverage is different from homeowner insurance, which guards against home damage losses.

<u>4. Minimum Down-Payment = 3.5%</u>

As just stated, the down-payment is 3.5% of the purchase price. If a house is contracted for $150,000, the down-payment is $5,250 ($150,000 * 3.5%). This money can come from:

- ✓ Verifiable gift funds;
- ✓ Checking, savings, certificates of deposits, money market accounts, mutual funds, stocks;
- ✓ Retirement accounts, such as 401k;
- ✓ Documented private savings clubs;
- ✓ Approved down-payment assistance programs;
- ✓ The sale of personal property.

The lender will verify the down-payment and its source during the loan application process.

Assistance programs are discussed in more detail in an upcoming section.

5. Credit Scores

Scores can be very low for FHA approval, with lender requirements being in the 600s. Meeting this standard will be easy if you are following the information presented in the *Credit Score to 700* book.

6. Debt-to-Income (DTI)

As of the writing of this book, average FHA debt-to-income (DTI) requisites are 31/43. The new house payment should not exceed 31% of gross income (called the front-end ratio). The projected mortgage payment, plus monthly consumer debts, should not exceed 43% (known as the back-end ratio).

Consumer debts referred to for calculating the back-end ratio are mortgage, installment, and revolving accounts – those items that are listed on the credit reports. However, other non-reporting monthly obligations -

such as alimony and child support – must also be considered.

Assume your annual income is $55,000, and monthly consumer debts total $1,200. The loan officer has stated that the new house payment - principal, interest, taxes, insurance (PITI) - will be $1,100/month.

According to FHA guidelines, the monthly house note should not exceed $1,420.83 (($55,000/12 months)*31%). Since the new payment of $1,100 is far less than the cutoff amount of $1,420.83, the front-end is good.

The proposed monthly house and consumer debt payments should not exceed $1,970.83 (($55,000/12)*43%). Let's check to see if it does.

Examine the following:

Gross Annual Income	$55,000
Monthly Income	**$4,583.33**
Auto Loan	$475
Credit Card 1	75
Credit Card 2	90
Furniture	120
Student Loan	440
Monthly Debts	**$1,200**
Proposed Mortgage	**$1,100**
Proposed Monthly Payout	**$2,300**
($1,200+1,100)	
Front-End Target - 31%	**$1,420.83**
(4,583*.31)	
Back-End Target - 43%	**$1,970.83**
(4,583*.43)	

The example shows that the proposed new mortgage and monthly debts total $2,300

(1,100 + 1,200). <u>This payout is higher than the maximum allowable 43% back-end of $1970.83.</u>

At this point, it seems like you do not qualify for the loan. The front-end ratio is less than 31%. It is 24% (1,100/4,583) and that is excellent. However, the back-end result is slightly over 50% (2,300/4,583). In this case, you will need guidance from your loan officer.

A back-end ratio of 50%, is not an automatic disqualification. Extenuating circumstances may prevail that still allows qualifying for the loan. For one thing, FHA loans have been known to close with back-ends as high as 50%. Nevertheless, this is not a good idea.

What the 50% back-end translates to is <u>half</u> of your monthly <u>gross</u> income will be going towards debt payments. Think about that, <u>not the take-home pay</u>, but **<u>gross income</u>**. A scenario like this could put you back on a bankruptcy path, and that is not wanted.

But what if you only have eight auto loan payments left? Then this liability would be excluded from the back-end equation. Installment debts with 10 or fewer payments remaining can be omitted. Other scenarios might prevail, as well.

The mortgage professional will know all the 'tricks of the trade.' Since you are still a little away from applying for the actual loan, work on reducing monthly obligations.

Another solution would be to find a less costly house that would allow both ratios to be acceptable.

7. Closing Cost

The seller can contribute up to 6% of the purchase price towards closing cost. However, you are not permitted to increase the offer amount to get the 6% on the back end. We will discuss closing cost items later in this book.

8. Loan Limits

The current FHA loan limits for single-family homes range from $314,827 to $726,525, depending on the county of your new residence. For instance, a single-family home in Madison, Wisconsin has a standard loan limit of $314,827, while a county in New York, New York has a maximum of $726,525.

Two-four family units have much higher limits. Ask your bank or loan officer about the maximum loan amount in your county of interest; FHA changes them almost yearly.

9. Reserve Requirements

So that you do not spend your last dime on a home purchase, there is a requirement that a certain amount is left over in an account after closing. These funds are called cash reserves.

For a single-family home, the reserve amount is one to two months of payments. To be safe, you should target at least three, if possible. For example, if the proposed monthly mortgage payment - principal, interest, taxes, and insurance (PITI) - is $1,100, you will need to show at least $1,100 - $2,200 left in savings, checking, or an acceptable investment account.

The lender will inform you of the expected cash reserve amount. If the purchase is a multi-unit dwelling, the requirement will be higher.

VA Requirements

1. Type of borrower

VA loans are for eligible military service members and their families.

2. Income Verification and Debt-to-Income (DTI)

The organization does not have established income or DTI conditions; nevertheless, lenders do.

3. Credit Score

No score is required. Again, the creditor will have a minimum standard.

4. Funding Fee

The VA demands an upfront funding fee (which is often financed in the mortgage). Although guidelines dictate the fee amount, the average is 2.15% of the loan.

5. Down-payment

VA loans are 100%; no down-payment required.

6. Seller Contribution

The seller can contribute up to 4% towards closing cost.

7. Loan Limit

As of the writing of this book, the limit for a single-family home is $484,350 for most counties. It is higher for more expensive areas. Again, ask the mortgage person to verify the maximum amount for your area; especially if you will be living in a high-cost community such as Anchorage, Alaska, Los Angeles, California, or New York, New York.

8. General Information

The service-connected profile is the first eligibility requirement. However, a dishonorable discharge will prohibit qualification under this program. The qualifying status is listed on DD Form 214.

For military actives, the statement of service and related records are evaluated to determine entitlement.

9. Cash Reserves

Although the VA does not have targeted numbers, it does encourage cash reserves.

Food for thought:

Since the VA's guides are a little vague, you should be in good shape by following applicable FHA parameters.

Notes

Foreclosure
Deed–in-Lieu
Short Sale

Chapter 6

Mortgage Included in Bankruptcy

(Foreclosure, Deed-In-Lieu, Short-Sale, Modification)

Often when individuals declare bankruptcy, they are forced to make detrimental housing decisions. They could have had their home go into foreclosure; submitted a deed-in-lieu; sold on a short sale; or even completed a loan modification. If any of these depicts your previous situation, you may have to wait past the two-year mark before being eligible to buy.

During a foreclosure, the bank forcibly takes back the property. Deed-in-lieu is when you offer the house to the bank before it forecloses. The lender allowing the property to be sold for less than what is owed defines a short sale. A loan modification is when the bank restructures the current loan so that it becomes more affordable. Unlike an elected refinance, restructuring is a direct result of financial hardship.

Each mortgage situation carries a different amount of weight and forgiveness period. A foreclosure may dictate three years before a new home purchase under FHA. The VA, which is much more forgiving, accepts the same bankruptcy waiting period of two years.

If you experienced one of these negative mortgage situations, refer to your loan officer for guidance.

Notes

Chapter 7

How Much House Can I Afford?

Since you have decided to own a home in two years, strive to be 'credit' and 'financially' ready. First, determine your affordable mortgage amount.

Although the upcoming calculations are examples only, they will allow you to become familiar with the financial end of the home buying process. Remember, at this point, you are merely looking ahead.

Two years from now will be too late to start addressing the financial end. Remember, have a plan and begin immediately. Work on credit and monetary situations from day one.

To determine your affordable maximum sales price, the lender reviews four main factors:

- Gross income;
- Monthly consumer debts;

- Debt-to-income ratios;
- FHA or VA loan limits.

Although, you can only predict your future financial state, try to be as exact as possible. This estimation will assist in providing a clearer picture of what is needed to make your dream a reality.

Also, since you are in the credit rebuilding phase, we will have to guess at the consumer debts at the time of loan application. When you are four-to-six months from applying for the mortgage, re-run the upcoming scenario. By that time, the figures should be more precise.

Gross Income

The gross income is earnings before any deductions. As previously stated, W2's, paystubs, and/or tax documents are used for this calculation. If you are self-employed or 1099, add the two adjusted gross figures from the previous two tax statements, then divide by 2 to determine the qualifying amount.

Example, the first tax statement shows adjusted gross income as $62,500. The second return displays $74,000. The qualifying income is $68,250 (($62,500+74,000)/2).

Better still, give the tax documents to your loan officer and let her determine the amount. Often self-employed, or 1099, returns and accompanying schedules are reviewed for write-offs and other income impacting items.

For this section, let's assume that your gross income = $75,000.

Gross Income	Yearly	Monthly
W2's, Paystubs, or Tax Returns	$75,000	$6,250

Monthly Debts

Your credit shows the following monthly debts. There are no other consumer payouts during the month than what is on the three reports.

Monthly Consumer Debts	
Auto Payment	$450
Credit Card 1	75
Credit Card 2	50
Furniture	45
Student Loan	$150
Total	$770

*Although you may have essential bills such as utilities, cell phone, and cable; these items are only considered for approval in non-institutional situations. Again, if you have no scores and trade lines on your reports, the lender could manually underwrite the loan by evaluating these payouts.

Debt-to-Income (DTI)

Debt-to-income is a primary factor. As listed in Chapter 5 (FHA Requirements: Debt-to-Income), evaluated debts are the consumer bills. The lender calculates front-end and back-end ratios to determine the impact of these liabilities.

As a refresher, the front-end ratio is the percentage of gross income that is going towards the "new" house payment. The back-end ratio is the percentage of gross income that represents the new house payment plus consumer debts. This one shows whether the total liabilities will pose a financial hardship.

Again, the targeted ratios for FHA are front-end - 31%, back-end - 43%. Actual front-end and back-end debts should not exceed these two percentages. Therefore, with a monthly gross income of $6,250 and consumer debt of $770, your front-end should not be greater than $1,937.50; while the back-end maximum is $2,687.50:

Gross Monthly Income * Ratio = Maximum Allowable Amount

Front-End - $6,250*.31 = $1,937.50

Back-End - $6,250*.43 = $2,687.50

<u>Since you have not started looking for a house and are more interested in approximates</u>, we will use your back-end results to determine the qualifying amount.

Again, the monthly consumer debts total $770, while the back-end maximum is $2,687.50. Therefore, your qualifying monthly mortgage is:

$2,687.50 – 770 = **$1,917.50**

Because $1,917.50 is less than the previously established front-end maximum of $1,937.50, you now know that your new monthly payment (PITI) should be $1,917.50 or less.

The next question is, what sales amount will equate to this monthly payment? Principal and interest are easier to determine than property taxes and homeowner's insurance. For this exercise, we will assume a property tax rate of 1.50% and insurance of .60%. I based these percentages on my housing costs. Of course, your actual amounts will differ.

The cost of taxes and insurance is different for each property. A county's Assessor calculates the tax amount through annual assessments. However, hazard insurance cost is determined by house size, structure, amount of coverage, etc. - even your credit can have an impact. Get quotes from at least two or three companies before making your purchasing decision.

The figures that I have provided will at least put you in the ballpark. At this point, we are merely trying to establish financial targets. Again, your mortgage professional can assist in estimating these two figures.

I am sure the burning question is still "how much house can I buy that totals $1,917.50/month or less?"

Let's analyze some FHA single-family home examples (VA payments will be less because you do not have the monthly mortgage insurance fee). We will examine three sales price scenarios - $200,000, $250,000, and $300,000.

(a)	Sales Prices	$200,000	$250,000	$300,000
(b)	Downpayment (FHA) - 3.5%	$7,000	$8,750	$10,500
(c)	**Base Loan Amount**	**$193,000**	**$241,250**	**$289,500**
(d)	Upfront Mort Ins - 1.75%	$3,378	$4,222	$5,066
(e)	**Total Loan Amount**	**$196,378**	**$245,472**	**$294,566**
(f)	Monthly Mort Insurance (Base Loan *.85%)/12	$136.71	$170.89	$205.06
(g)	Principal and Interest (Current Fixed Rates - 4.50%)	$995.02	$1,243.77	$1,492.52
(h)	Taxes (Estimate - 1.5%)	$250.00	$312.50	$375.00
(i)	Insurance (estimate - .60%)	$100.00	$125.00	$150.00
(j)	**Estimated Monthly Payment**	**$1,481.73**	**$1,852.16**	**$2,222.58**

(a) Again, we randomly selected three sales prices for our analysis – $200,000, $250,000, and $300,000.

(b) The FHA down-payment requirement is 3.5% (example: $200,000 * 3.5% = $7,000).

(c) The base loan amount that you will be seeking from the lender is the sales price minus the down-payment ($200,000 – 7,000 = $193,000).

(d) As of the writing of this book, FHA requires an upfront mortgage insurance fee of 1.75% of the base loan amount (193,000*1.75% = $3,378).

(e) Total loan amount is computed by adding upfront mortgage insurance to the base loan amount ($193,000+3,378 = $196,378).

(f) FHA also demands monthly mortgage insurance payments against the base loan amount. At a down-payment of 3.5%, your monthly premium will be at least .85% (please note that other factors could increase this percentage). For this scenario we will go with .85% (($193,000*.85%)/12 = $136.71/month).

(g) Pretend that your lender is offering a mortgage interest rate of 4.5% for a fixed 30-year period. Your principal and interest for the total loan amount of $196,378 for 30 years = $995.02/month (you can determine this payment by using any mortgage calculator. Try one offered by the Navy Federal Credit Union website or bankrate.com).

(h) I estimated 1.5% for the taxes - which is my payment percentage. Again, your tax rate will be different based on your county's assessment – check with a local real estate agent or your loan officer. The percentage will be multiplied against the sales price, not the loan amount ($200,000 * 1.5% = $3,000; 3,000/12 = $250/month).

(i) Hazardous insurance fee comes from the insurance company that you select and their criteria. For this example, I used .60% (my rate). Again, check with an insurance professional

($200,000*.60% = $1,200;
$1,200/12=$100/month).

(j) Your monthly mortgage payment at $200,000 is $1,481.73 (Mortgage Insurance = $136.71; principal and interest = $995.02; taxes = $250.00; hazard insurance = $100.00)

As you can see, at a sales price of $200,000, your monthly payment of $1,481.73 is way less than your maximum qualifying amount of $1,917.50. You could qualify for a larger home purchase. Therefore, analyze the scenarios at $250,000 and $300,000.

The calculations indicate that you should be able to qualify for a sales price at $250,000 ($1,852.16/month), but not $300,000 ($2,222.58/month). At $250,000, your DTI ratios would be:

Front-End – 1,852.16/6,250 = 30%

Back-End – (1,852.16+770(consumer debts))/6,250 = 42%

With this scenario, your DTI ratios are less than the FHA required maximums of 31% and 43%.

Since the lender only examines the proposed mortgage, along with the monthly consumer debts to qualify you for your new home; you may want to go one step further and consider all possible monthly payouts.

These obligations include groceries, gas, utilities, cell phone, Homeowner Association fees (HOA), lawn care, cable, and auto insurance. This evaluation will consider all of your monthly expenses, including the new house payment; before you make an offer to buy. You will not be shocked after you are in the house and obligated to pay the new living expenses.

What can work to offset this shock is the tax benefits that come along with owning a home. Speak with a tax accountant to see how much more you can bring home in each paycheck. Tax information is also available at www.irs.gov.

Loan Limits

As previously stated, FHA and VA have loan limits. The ceiling amounts are county-based. For instance, if you will be buying a single-family home in Atlanta, Georgia (Fulton County), the FHA limit is $314,827, while VA is $484,350. Again, contact the respective governing agency (FHA/VA) or your loan officer to clarify the maximum for the county where you will be residing.

For the previous scenario, your qualifying sales price of $250,000 is well below the limit for any county in the country.

Food for thought

If you decide on a housing sales price of $200,000 ($1,481.73/month) instead of one at $250,000 ($1,852.16/month), the savings would be $370.43/month (1,852.16 – 1,481.73). Imagine what you could do with the extra cash.

Just because you qualify to buy at a specific maximum price, does not mean that you must purchase at that amount. Your past economic hardship (bankruptcy) dictates thinking and acting conservatively on all financial matters.

Also, do not automatically select a fixed rate mortgage. If the plan is to live in the house for only five years, then a 5-year ARM is the best choice. It provides a smaller monthly payment because the interest rate will be lower than a fixed one. With a 5/1-ARM, there is no adjustment until after five years; seven and ten-year ARM's are also available.

However, if you are planning to remain in the home indefinitely, or are uncertain about the time frame, then a fixed rate may be a better choice. Be sure to discuss the various rate scenarios with your lender or loan officer. Compare the pros and cons of each type before making a final decision. If an ARM is selected, be sure that you are comfortable with the projected payment increases.

Chapter 8

How Much Money Will I Need?

For this section, we will be using the qualifying amount of $250,000 discussed in the last chapter.

Once you find your dream home and offer a contract, there will be out-of-pocket costs. These fees are incurred at contract offer, during the approval process, and loan closing. The question is - how much money is needed?

Cost varies, from the binder fee to the closing table. No two buyers will have the same obligation. However, this book will assist with providing a close estimate (no guarantee).

Earnest Money (Binder Fee)

Earnest money is required with the sales offer. It binds the contract and shows all parties that you are serious. Once an offer is accepted, the binder fee becomes a part of the down-payment.

This cost is often $500 to $1,000; sometimes even higher than that. However, I have never offered nor had a client to give more than $1,000. Of course, if you are trying to buy a $500,000 or $1,000,000 house, you may have to present more. Your real estate agent will assist with this.

Although the binder converts to down-payment at closing, it bears some risks. If you do not complete the requirements of the contract, you could lose the earnest money.

For example, if you change your mind about purchasing the property after the contract has been signed by all parties, you will probably lose the binder. Therefore, it is best to offer the smallest acceptable amount.

Home Inspection

A home inspection should uncover any hidden defects. Although this is optional, the contract does provide a certain number of days to get the property inspected. If you do not know a qualified inspector, ask your agent for a referral.

She or her broker may have a list of professionals that they employ regularly. Go one step further and research reviews on any inspector and his company.

I advise you to have an inspection completed on the selected house. You want to know everything that is wrong with the property before purchasing it. What if the home needs a new roof or a major wood-destroying infestation exists? Do not skip this vital process.

However, be aware that home inspection is also an upfront expense. It normally cost $350-$500. Once the process is complete, the agent negotiates for the seller to make some or all repairs. If an agreement is unable to be reached about who will bear the repair costs, you can terminate and walk away from the contract.

Unfortunately, if the deal does fall apart, the money you spent on the inspection is not recoverable. Think about it like this - it is best to risk this cash, rather than to find out later that you are on the hook for a $6,000 roof replacement or in need of all new plumbing?

Even worse, what if the electrical wiring is faulty? You get the picture. The money paid is worth the peace of mind when compared to the potential costs of looming defects.

Have a budget for the property evaluation of at least $500. If you are buying a large house, this fee could be higher.

Also, be present for the inspection. You want to witness that the professional is checking all areas of the house. Be curious and ask questions.

The last thing you want is to receive an inspection report from someone who spent little time examining the property. Any defects that are missed will come back to haunt you later. After closing, all repairs are your responsibility.

Appraisal Fee

Another cost requirement is the upfront appraisal fee. Before the deal settles, the bank will require that you pay for a property appraisal. The lender selects the company and orders the assessment; however, you bear the cost.

You and the lender want to be comfortable that the value of the property you are buying is at least equal to the contracted amount. If not, terminate the deal or complete an amendment that will lower the sales price. The average appraisal cost is $500.

Homeowner's Insurance Policy

Shortly before the bank provides settlement instructions, it will require you to purchase a year's coverage of homeowner's insurance. For this exercise, we assumed a policy cost of .60% of the sales price ($250,000*.60% = $1,500/year). Be aware that the lender will also add at least two monthly payments to the settlement charges ($1500/12*2 = $250).

Down-Payment

As previously stated, the VA does not have a down-payment requirement; however, FHA does. It is 3.5% of the sales price. In our example, the charge is $8,750 ($250,000*3.5%). The money can come from various approved sources.

Some state and local agencies have available down-payment assistance programs. Unlike commercial deals, the funds are not required to be repaid if certain conditions are met. These terms include:

- ✓ Completing a home buying education seminar;
- ✓ Remaining in the "new" home for a required number of years;
- ✓ Being at or below a certain income level;
- ✓ Being a first-time homebuyer;
- ✓ Purchasing in a specific geographical location, etc.

Available down-payment resources include fha.com, state programs, and the National Council of State Housing Agencies.

FHA.com

I accessed a list of programs from www.fha.**com** – "Down Payment Assistance Programs for Homebuyers." Although I cannot guarantee or endorse any of the listings, you should research and discuss them with your loan officer.

My advice is to stay clear of any that has a repayment feature. The payback requirement would add a new debt that could hurt your overall mortgage qualifying chances.

Again, retrieve the list from fha.com (which is not the government site - fha.gov). Available programs are displayed by state, on this website. For Georgia, it shows *Georgia Dream Homeownership Program* (https://www.dca.ga.gov) and *Homestretch Down Payment Assistance Program* (https://www.gwinnettcounty.com/static/departments/financialservices/hud_grants/nsp/2018/2018-%20Gwinnett%20County%20Homestretch%20Pre-Application.pdf.).

State Programs

Georgiadownpaymentassistance.com is another site that displays resources for that state's residents. It includes "Atlanta Affordable Homeownership Program (AAHOP)," "Invest Atlanta," and "Dekalb County Home Down Payment Assistance Program."

Complete a web search for available programs in your state. For example, in your Google search bar type, "Downpayment Assistance Programs in (*type your state's name*).” It is well worth the time. Again, a mortgage professional can assist with this effort.

<u>*NCSHA*</u>

The National Council of State Housing Agencies (NCSHA) is another resource that identifies funds for mortgages and down-payment assistance. Among its offerings are government-backed tax-exempt Mortgage Revenue Bonds (MRB) and “HOME Investment Partnerships Program.”

For more details, go to www.ncsha.org, email info@ncsha.org, or call (202) 624-7710.

Closing Costs

As previously stated, once at the loan closing, there will be settlement charges. These fees, which are estimates during the pre-approval phase, become actuals.

The following is an example of closing expenses. Again, as in all cases, the actual amounts will differ; even the item list may not be the same. Use the data provided as a guide only.

Closing Cost ($250,000 Sale):	
Down-payment (minus $1000 binder)	$7,750
Lender Fees and Points - 1.5% (of Loan Amt)	3,682
Credit Report	50
Flood Certificate	75
Tax Service	175
Title Services (all)	1,500
Government Recording	25
Attorney Fee	500
Wire Fee	50
Recording Fee	250
Transfer Taxes	1,200
Hazard Ins (2 mos)	250
Taxes (6 mos)	1,875
Total Closing Cost	**$17,382**

This list is not exclusive, nor all-inclusive, there could be other fees. The amounts will vary, as well. Refer to the 'Sales Price' table presented in Chapter 7 to determine how we calculated the down-payment, hazard insurance, and taxes.

The closing costs for our example totals $17,382.

Seller Contribution

To assist with the settlement charges of $17,382, both FHA and VA permit seller contribution. FHA allows up to 6% of the sales price, while the VA permits 4%. In our FHA loan scenario, the seller can contribute up to $15,000 ($250,000*.06). Your mortgage professional will be able to tell you which expenses can be paid by the seller.

As you can see, it is a good idea to engage your loan officer in the process as early as possible. At a minimum, she can research tax information; check on available down-payment assistance; provide insurance company and property inspector lists; as well as, prepare a closing cost estimate. After you apply for the loan, she will give you an official Good Faith Estimate (GFE), which is more precise.

Finally, the seller's contribution to closing costs is not automatic nor guaranteed. Your real estate agent will need to ask for it in the sales offer. If accepted, it becomes a part of the final contract.

However, you cannot receive more than the closing amount. For instance, if the seller contribution is $15,000 and the costs total $12,000 – you will only receive the allowable sum up to $12,000. Make sure that you see the contribution amount or percentage listed in the offer, before it is presented to the seller.

I once had an agent who tried to ask for 1%; I insisted that she change the figure - which she did hesitantly. Guess what, the seller agreed to my closing cost percentage. Had I not been adamant, I would have been paying thousands more out of pocket to settle the deal.

Reserves

As previously stated, the FHA has a reserve requirement. It is one-to-two months of monthly payments for a single-family home.

However, you do not need to bring this amount to the closing table; it just needs to be in a certifiable account before the deal settles. Using the 'new' home monthly payment amount in the 'Sales Price' example from Chapter 7, you will need $3,704.32 (1,852.16 *2) left over in an account.

Total Out-of-Pocket Cost

For the $250,000 purchase example, your expected out-of-pocket would be:

(a) $9,632 – Closing costs to settle the deal ($17,382 minus the down-payment amount and earnest money – which are listed below)

(b) $7,750 - Down-payment

(c) Upfronts (out-of-pocket before closing) - \$3,500

\$1,000 – Earnest money (credited to down-payment at closing)

\$500 – Home inspection

\$500 – Appraisal fee

\$1,500 – 1st-year homeowner's policy cost

(d) Reserves after closing – \$3,704.32 (two mortgage payments)

Grand Total = \$24,586.32

What? That is a Lot of Money

I am sure that after seeing these figures, your mind is on overload. You are probably thinking to yourself, "This is a lot of money. How can I come up with this amount in 24 months?"

Trust me, when I tell you that there are ways besides working yourself to death. Let's pretend that the following happens for this FHA deal (which are possible):

1) Your agent will cover the bulk of the closing costs by asking the seller to contribute 6%. Again, this must be included in the initial written offer and agreed upon by both parties. For the presented scenario, we are going to assume that all the closing costs will come from the seller. He will contribute $9,632. The max is $15,000 ($250,000*6%).

2) You qualify for a down-payment assistance program that covers the $8,750 (at closing, you will receive credit for the $1,000 paid in earnest money).

3) You will need $3,500 for your upfront fees, which are an appraisal, inspection, homeowner's insurance, and earnest money.

4) After closing, two mortgage payments totaling $3,704.32 should still be in an account.

Based on the scenario presented, which is possible (not guaranteed), the total out of pocket is $3,500 – which are the upfront costs. However, you still need to show the reserve amount ($3,704.32) in your bank account.

But what if the lender requires only one month of cash? Then the reserve will be only $1,852.16 ($3,704.32÷2). To be safe, assume that the lender will ask for two months.

Since the purchase is two years away, have as much money as possible - go beyond $7,204.32 ($3,500 + $3,704.32). What if you are unable to get down-payment assistance? Then that amount would need to come from you, as well. Remember, obtaining down-payment assistance is doable.

Final note, although FHA allows the seller to contribute up to 6%, it may require that certain items be paid only by the buyer. If this is the case, you would then have to cover those amounts, as well. In the past, these totaled a few hundred dollars.

Again, an experienced loan officer can determine some of the charges even when you are in the credit rebuilding phase. She will be able to guide you from day one.

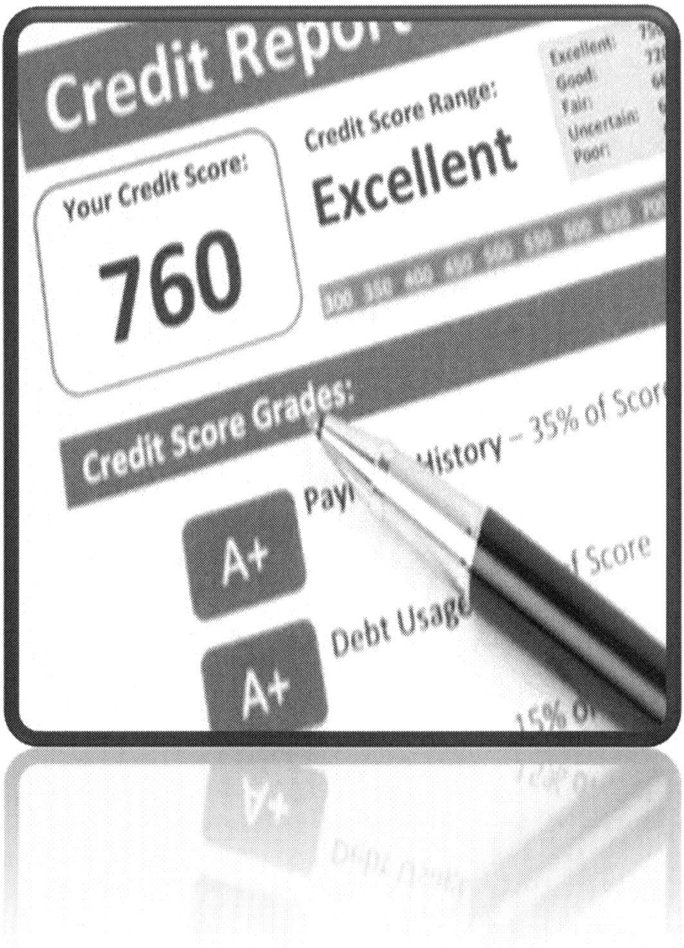
Credit Score Range:
Excellent
Your Credit Score:
760
Credit Score Grades:
A+
A+

Chapter 9

18-22 Months After Discharge

It has been 18 months since the discharge. You have repaired your credit and managed to save for the purchase. Remember, you should be able to get pre-approved for the home loan after the 2nd anniversary of the discharge date. Now at six months away, double-check to ensure that everything is on track.

You should:

- Re-pull your credit from the three bureaus;
- Dispute any inaccuracies that may have crept back on the report(s);
- Ensure that the new credit accounts are reporting your excellent payment history;

- Retrieve your last two federal income taxes and W2's;

- Check on existing funds and any other sources. Be confident that the money is available or will be by month 21. The mortgage company will ask for the last two bank and investment statements during the loan application process.

If Aunt Grace has promised money for the down-payment, try to deposit it in month 21 – at the latest. If your statement shows a substantial deposit when the bank reviews it, the lender will want to know the source of the funds.

They may also seek bank records from Aunt Grace and even try to determine how she got the money. This request is called source and seasoning. Where did the funds come from and how long have you had them?

To avoid this hassle, have the money in your account at least three to four months before the loan process begins. When the lender requests two months of bank statements, he can see that the required funds are already in your account. If you are obtaining down-payment assistance from an organization, then source and seasoning will not apply. You can receive this donation much later in the process.

CASHBOOK

Chapter 10

23-24 Months After Discharge

You are now in the home stretch. You checked your credit and did have to make a few more disputes. All updates are complete, and you are getting closer to the actual home buying phase. From this period through closing:

- Do not transfer funds between accounts. This action may prompt the lender to ask for more paperwork showing where the money was initially, as well as, why the transfer;

- Do not make any large deposits or withdrawals unless you can provide a written explanation.

Also, by now, you should have or start looking for a real estate agent. Ask friends, family, and co-workers for referrals.

Interview at least two people. Are they full-time or part-time? If part-time, what is the schedule for showing properties? How many closings have they had? If they are new to the business, are they affiliated with a reputable broker?

Be comfortable with the selection and confident that she will work in your best interest. Also, know that in most cases, the seller pays the agent. Although you may have selected her, unless you employ a buyer's agent, she works for the seller.

Only divulge personal and financial information to your loan officer. Your agent does not need to know your income. She merely needs to be aware of the approved sales amount and your housing requirements.

At twenty-three months is also the time to start cruising your potential neighborhoods. Try to visit at least five areas that match the sales range and housing requirements. It is a good idea to visit these places at various times to get a feel for activity in the mornings, evenings, nights, and weekends. Visit after it rains to ensure that a flood issue is not present.

For comparison, ask your agent to provide neighborhood overviews. The report should indicate demographics, the number of homes in each area, buy/sell activity, crime rates; as well as schools and their ratings. The proximity to work, grocery, restaurants, and shopping may also be of interest to you.

Things to Consider

The shows on HGTV can familiarize you with the house hunting process, especially *House Hunters*. This television show is one of my favorites. The issues that these people encounter are very real.

Just like the buyers on TV, your considerations include:

- ✓ House style (cape cod, traditional, colonial, contemporary);

- ✓ Ranch, two-story, split-foyer, split-level;
- ✓ Single-family, duplex, triplex, multi-unit;
- ✓ Townhome, condominium;
- ✓ Year built;
- ✓ Garage - single, double, or three-car;
- ✓ Square footage;
- ✓ Lot size;
- ✓ Number of bedrooms;
- ✓ Number of bathrooms;
- ✓ Laundry room or closet;
- ✓ Separate pantry;
- ✓ Finished basement;
- ✓ Den;
- ✓ Number of fireplaces;
- ✓ Formal living room;
- ✓ Dining room or eat-in kitchen;
- ✓ Open concept;
- ✓ Separate home office;
- ✓ Large kitchen with an island or a galley;
- ✓ Yard size;
- ✓ Pool, deck, or patio;
- ✓ View;
- ✓ Daily commute time.

This list contains numerous considerations. Determine your 'must haves' versus 'wants.' Furthermore, be realistic in your demands. You might want a 3,000 sq.ft. home, but your budget may only allow for a 2,000.

In addition to HGTV, other homebuying resources are zillow.com, trulia.com, and realty.com. These sites also provide square footage, lot sizes, HOA information, demographics, and crime data.

Start Gathering Documents

During the pre-approval and loan application phases, the loan officer will request various documents from each borrower (sometimes more than once). She is going to ask for:

- ✓ Most recent 30 days of paystubs;
- ✓ Last 2-years of W2's or 1099's;
- ✓ Two-years of tax returns;
- ✓ Last two months of checking and saving statements – all pages;

- ✓ Most recent investment statements – 401k, Stocks, Mutual Fund, IRA;
- ✓ Official photo i.d. and social security card;
- ✓ Divorce decree or marriage certificate;
- ✓ Court-ordered child support and alimony documents;
- ✓ Bankruptcy discharge letter;
- ✓ Current landlord (or mortgage company) address and contact information;
- ✓ Employer Human Resources address and contact information;
- ✓ DD-214 – Condition of military discharge;
- ✓ Gift letter, along with proof of gift funds;
- ✓ Proof of social security or retirement income;
- ✓ Business Profit and Loss statement.

This list is not all-inclusive. These are just some of the documents that may be required. Note that once you have a signed contract, you will also be asked for the:

- ✓ Purchase and Sales Agreement – including all attachments;
- ✓ Earnest money check - front and back copies.

The bank may also request a letter of explanation regarding the nature of your bankruptcy.

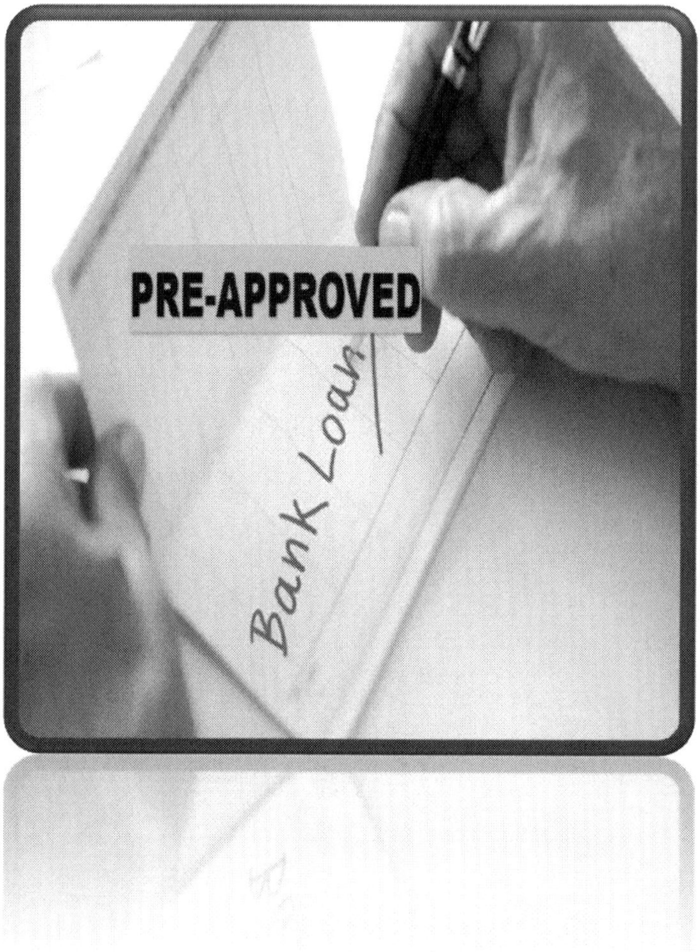
PRE-APPROVED
Bank Loan

Chapter 11

It Is Your 2nd Anniversary

After the 2nd anniversary of the discharge date, you are ready to get formally pre-approved for a loan. The house buying process officially begins. If you have followed the ideas presented in this book, prepare for a drama-free ride; at least on your side of the fence.

<u>Make sure that you receive a pre-approval, not a prequalification</u>. Pre-approvals are more detailed. For pre-quals, the lender merely asks a few questions about your financials, then reviews one or two credit reports and scores. Based on that information, he provides the maximum purchase price.

As you can tell, the decision is based on limited data. What if during the formal loan application review, it is discovered that your income is less than you initially reported? What if you have more debt than is showing on the reports? With a pre-qual, there is a higher risk of not qualifying during the loan review.

With a pre-approval, the bank's evaluation is more detailed. You must provide income and financial statements. The lender examines all three credit reports and scores. Once you receive the purchase letter, the risk of not getting approved is minimized.

Be aware that the exact payment amount will not be known until after you submit the final application. The loan amount and interest rate determine the monthly mortgage's principal and interest charges.

Notes

Checklist
Yes
No

Chapter 12

Do's and Don'ts After Pre-Approval

With the pre-approval letter in hand, you are officially ready to begin house hunting. This document is the only thing that you will need to share with the real estate agent. Again, your financial information is provided to the loan officer only.

After you receive the pre-approval letter, follow the listed "do's" and "don'ts."

Do continue to:

- ✓ Pay your bills on time;
- ✓ Save money. The more assets you can show, the better;
- ✓ Provide requested documentation, promptly;
- ✓ Maintain bank account stability by not moving money (at least without your loan officer's knowledge);

- ✓ Keep credit accounts to 30% or less of the maximum amounts.

Don't:

- ✓ Buy anything using your credit, such as a car or furniture, until after your loan has closed;
- ✓ Change jobs without consulting your loan officer;
- ✓ Have your credit pulled by anyone other than the lender;
- ✓ Liquidate or close any bank or investment accounts;
- ✓ Open new credit accounts;
- ✓ Transfer credit card balances.

Another "do" is to remain focused and a part of the entire process. Although you will let the various professionals handle their business, know that this will be <u>your</u> investment. Therefore, trust - but verify.

Read and agree before you sign anything. Ask questions when you do not understand. Expect clear answers to those questions.

Once the entire process is over, only you will have to live with the outcome.

CONTRACT

Chapter 13

Home Searching

Since your list of neighborhood and home choices have narrowed over the past couple of months, you now are aware of the 'must haves.' No one house will have everything you are seeking – unless it is custom built. Because of this fact, keep an open mind.

As you view the various homes, your priorities could change. You may not find 100% of what you want, but a good compromise will be evident. Do not try to buy the biggest and most expensive house in a neighborhood. Your neighbors will benefit from your home value, not the other way around.

Also, you earn profits when a home is purchased, not when it is sold. Translation, if you buy at a reasonable price, you will make more money on the back end when you sell it.

Therefore, as part of the home search process, your real estate agent will provide data on houses that are comparable to the ones that you are considering. These homes should have the same characteristics – size, floor plan, number of rooms, etc. This information will assist in narrowing your choices and determining the final offer amount.

Also, the agent should research as much as she can about your chosen neighborhood and surrounding area. She will know if home prices have been increasing or decreasing over the past few years. The last thing you want to do is move into a declining community.

By the way, do not forget to check for railroad tracks and airplane flight paths. My very first purchase was across the street from a railroad track. I noticed it but did not consider the noise factor. I was young and naïve.

In the beginning, the trains were annoying. Soon I adjusted to the noise. However, I now know to consider such annoyances. You should be mindful of anything that impedes your quality of life, as well.

Likewise, inquire if the property is in a flood zone. Not only can this be problematic, but there will be a requirement to purchase more insurance. The flood policy would become an added expense.

Be sure to review other area data such as the crime rate, neighborhood income, demographics, and proposed changes. As previously stated, you are interested in a community <u>and</u> its surroundings.

make an
OFFER!

Chapter 14

Making the Offer

Again, before you make an offer to buy, double-check all expenses associated with owning the home – including the Homeowner Association (HOA) fee. This cost can be hundreds of dollars each month.

Also, ask the agent about contingencies. These are escape clauses in the contract that allow you to back out without losing money. They provide relief from certain "what if" situations.

Contingencies allow you to get out of the contract if:

- You are unable to obtain financing at a specified rate and term;
- The inspection report is unacceptable, or the seller does not agree to make requested repairs;

- There is evidence of termites or other wood-destroying pests;

- The home appraisal is less than the agreed upon sales price;

- An environmental hazard exists, such as radon gas;

- The loan does not close on the agreed date;

- The seller does not provide a one-year homeowner's warranty.

Most of these contingencies are automatically in the wording of the Purchase and Sales Agreement. Ask your agent to point them out. If any of the issues listed above becomes a reality, you will be able to terminate the contract and get your earnest money back. This list is not all-inclusive; these are the more common ones.

Furthermore, before making an offer, be sure that you are 100% comfortable with the deal - including the binder amount. If you are unable to fulfill the terms of the agreement, you could lose money.

Remember, there is no set amount for earnest money (unless you are buying a specially handled property, like a HUD foreclosure). For a regular sale, the binder should be $1,000 or less. Your agent will advise you about this matter.

When the sales proposal is presented to the sellers, they will have 24-48 hours to accept. Often the seller counteroffers, which is where the negotiating begins. Work closely with your agent to ensure that she is responding timely and accurately.

What if you change your mind after the offer is submitted? You can formally withdraw if it has <u>not</u> been signed by the seller. If it has, you may be able to exercise a contingency to get out of the deal.

If the seller has merely made a counteroffer, then do not accept it. Just let the response time expire. If the signed contract has not closed and you decide to withdraw, you risk losing your earnest money and being sued to complete the terms as defined in the sales agreement.

Do your due diligence and read the offer and counteroffers before you agree to the terms. Only you will have to live with the final executable contract. However, your agent and loan officer will work hard so that everything happens as expected.

Also, know what you are buying, do not assume. If the property comes with a washer and dryer, make sure that the items are in the agreement. Anything that is for sale with the house - furniture, drapery, ceiling fans, unique fixtures, etc. - should be itemized in the contract. If not, the seller could easily remove them.

My first purchase was a new townhome. The builder promised blinds, washer, dryer, stove, microwave, and refrigerator. The items were listed in the contract. Had they not been, I would not have had any recourse if the builder reneged.

Finally, included in the sales offer should be a request to complete a final walk-thru of the house within 24 hours of closing; after the seller has moved out. This inspection will ensure that you have had a chance to review the property and that there will be no surprises when you move in.

If you elect to close the deal before the seller moves out, add a clause or an addendum to the Purchase and Sales Agreement that will protect your investment.

Chapter 15

Closing the Deal

Today is the day that you have dreamed about for the past two years. By now, you should have already received the Settlement Statement (HUD-1), which lists the final monetary distributions. Examine the statement to be sure that everything is correct. Also, obtain a cashier's check for the amount that you are required to pay.

At the closing, understand the documents that you are signing. Ask questions about anything vague. At this point, the pressure is on, and everyone is anxious to make things happen.

I admit that very few people spend time reading every single line of the documents. Most rely on the attorney to explain each sheet as he encounters it. They merely sign where he points; which is not a good practice, but it happens. The interest is more in getting the keys, garage door openers, and all other items that come with the new house.

A week or two after the closing, contact your county tax assessor or commissioner's office to inquire about homestead exemption. If available, it will lower your annual property taxes; which translates to smaller monthly payments.

Notes

Chapter 16

Conclusion

Buying a home is the ultimate investment. Why? Because as you pay down the mortgage each month, the value of the house continues to increase. This appreciation can provide a financial return that exceeds any other investment that you will make in your lifetime. So why not seek this opportunity, even after bankruptcy?

Just because you have had a temporary financial setback, does not mean that you must sit on the sidelines for ten years and watch others make this dream a reality. It is possible to jump in the real estate game and own your first or another home within two years after bankruptcy. As Nike says, "just do it."

Made in the
USA
Columbia, SC

79314922R00065